about the auth

It's not every day you'll meet someone like

Giada is a bike messenger turned massage therapist. Her first practice was called the Massage Garage, and her title: The Body Mechanic.

After leaving Canada, she let the wind take her to where she is today, Galway, Ireland.

Giada has always followed her heart and resisted working the conventional 9-5. Ultimately, she prefers to work for herself, despite the challenges of being an entrepreneur.

In 2018, she started a corporate wellness company called OFFICE KNEADS and her own private practice called SHE KNEADS.

It is these practices, and her years of working as a massage therapist for office workers, busy parents, motor vehicle accident survivors and professional athletes, that inspired her to write this book.

Giada is a helper, a giver and a healer. She believes strongly in the power of natural medicine and therapies. Having been an office worker, an athlete, and a bus accident survivor herself, she understands pain and stress, and what it can do to a person not just physically, but mentally, emotionally and even spiritually.

It is her mission to bring about a stronger awareness and culture of wellness within the corporate world and beyond. She believes in empowering people with the knowledge to maintain themselves, while also educating her clients on the possibilities of natural therapies and holistic resources.

table of contents

introduction

If you've ever worked in an office, you're probably no stranger to the aches and pains of **#desklife**. Rumour has it that sitting is the new smoking and though that may seem like a gross exaggeration, there is some validity in it.

A sedentary lifestyle can lead to many physical problems. If left untreated or uncared for, these problems can become chronic conditions.

Another common issue in the workplace is repetitive strain. These are every day injuries that are caused by repeating the same movements over and over again without stretching or remedying the problems. An example of repetitive strain might be holding the phone with the same shoulder every time, causing an imbalance in the neck muscles and leading to neck tension and headaches.

Finally, it is a known fact that mental health is a leading cause of lost work days and has a massive impact on productivity loss, performance and cost.

In the following pages, you will find quick tips and tricks to help reduce and relieve pains, stresses and tensions, leaving you healthier, happier and more capable than ever before.

coffee or tea

Coffee and caffeinated teas are an office-crowd's favourite remedy for tiredness. On average, office workers drink 3+ cups a day.

While caffeine isn't dehydrating per se, it IS a mild diuretic, meaning it causes more frequent urination. It's important to replace the liquid you're losing, so remember to drink adequate amounts of clean water, as well as eat fruits and vegetables with a high water content such as oranges or cucumbers.

Did you know that black tea with no milk and sugar is a good **remedy for a hangover**?

Did you know that a pint of water first thing in the morning, and an apple right after, has the **energetic equivalence** of a cup of coffee?

The natural sugars and vitamins from the skin of an apple are released slowly in the body, making it a healthy alternative for wakefulness.

Herbal teas such as Chamomile and Peppermint are great tools for stress and anxiety relief. Both have calming effects on the nervous system and help to reduce muscle tension.

NOTE: Chamomile tea is a mild sedative and is known as a remedy for insomnia. Keep this in mind, as you may not want to be sleepy while at work.

tension headaches

Tension headaches are often a by-product of one of three things: **jaw clenching, eye-straining** or **sinus congestion**.

If you get one, here's what you can do:

jaw clenching

These tension headaches are felt in the sides of the head, in the jaw muscles and the temples.

Treating them is easy.

With your finger tips, apply tolerable pressure to the muscle along the jaw bone. Just below the cheekbone you will typically find a point of tension.

Slowly open and close the jaw.

This will effectively stretch the jaw muscles, and reduce tension in the head.

If jaw clenching is not addressed properly these headaches can eventually turn into neck and shoulder tension and possibly migraines.

> ! To reduce jaw tension, massage the cheeks and temples.

eye strain

Eye strain headaches are felt around the eyes, heaviness in the forehead, or as pain in the back of the head.

These headaches are often a result of staring at a screen for too long without breaks. They are especially likely if your computer screen is dirty.

To relieve eye strain, follow these three steps:

1. Rub your hands together to warm them.
2. Close your eyes and place your warm hands over them for thirty seconds. Do not apply pressure to the lids.
3. Slowly open your eyes and look around.

Tension headaches can ALSO be due to lack of sleep, dehydration or hunger.

NOTE: If you have a clean screen, and you don't spend too much time staring at one, but still find that you are having these headaches please make an appointment with an optometrist to check your vision.
You may need glasses, or a different prescription if you already have them.

sinus congestion

Your sinuses come in the form of four hollow cavities in the skull that connect to the nasal pathways and are lined with a mucous membrane.

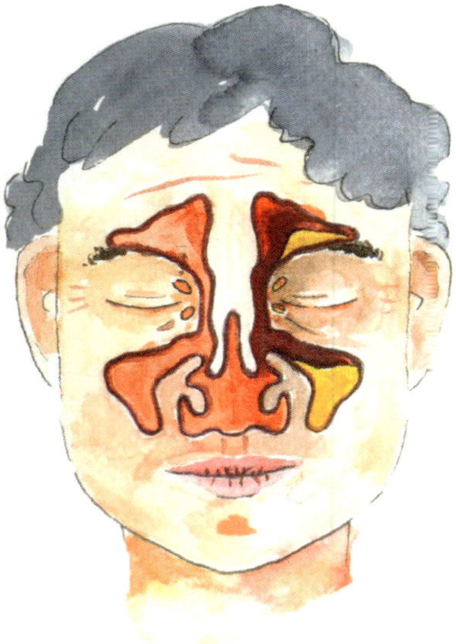

For various reasons, like allergies for instance, these mucous membranes become inflamed and the cavities fill with fluid and do not empty, causing congestion.

Sinus congestion can be extremely frustrating and will often cause sinus headaches. These headaches are felt as a pressure in the face and forehead which can worsen when lying down, and are not relieved by simply blowing the nose.

To help relieve the pressure and clear the congestion,
I suggest three things: **Massaging, Tapping and Vibrating.**

The idea is to encourage circulation and movement in these congested areas.

What you'll find is that after a few minutes of using these techniques, your nose will unblock itself and you will be able to blow your nose and maybe even breathe properly.

Depending on the reason for your congestion, you may need to use this technique a few times. It might not always work, but when it does, be sure to have some tissues on hand.

Note: Regularly consuming local honey works wonders for hay fever and pollen allergies.

neck & shoulder tension

What you are about to read will LITERALLY change you physically.

Ready?

Here it is:

A major reason for neck and shoulder tension is poor posture.

Between slumped shoulders and imbalanced neck muscles, it's no wonder most of us walk around with chronic neck and shoulder tension.

The truth is, if left untreated, poor posture gets worse over time, leading to mild to severe structural deformities, such as hyperkyphosis (hunch back) and scoliosis (S-curved spine).

The GOOD news

You can reduce and even potentially prevent these problems with a few simple stretches that can be done in less than five minutes, right at your desk.

But first, let me tell you a bit about the neck muscle group known as the...

scalenes

The scalenes are a group of muscles found mirrored on either side of your throat.

The Scalene muscles become tight over time from shallow breathing, stress, tension, and looking down for prolonged periods of time (like looking down at your phone or laptop, for instance).

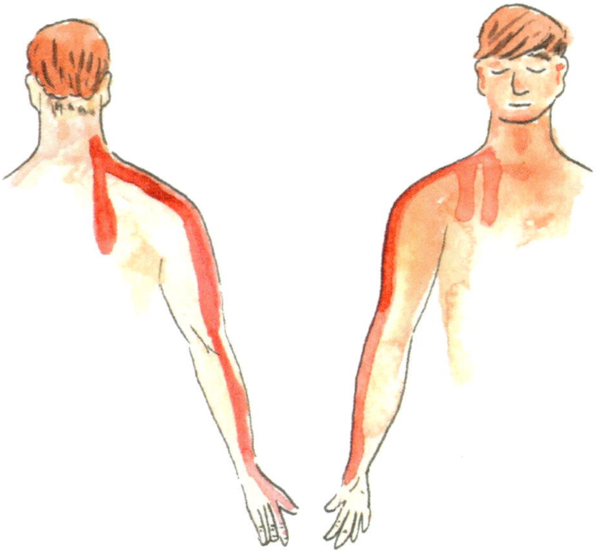

When these muscles become tight, a few things can happen. First it creates an imbalance with the muscles in the back of your neck, resulting in a strain in your upper back, neck and shoulders.

In severe cases, tight Scalenes can result in Thoracic Outlet Syndrome (TOS) which is commonly experienced as pain in the neck and shoulders, and numbness or tingling in the arms or fingers.

So what can you do to impede these avoidable pains?

scalenes stretch

To stretch the scalene muscles, follow these two steps:

STEP 1

Bring right-hand fingers to your right collar bone (slightly above).

Look down to the elbow.

STEP 2

Apply pressure just above the collar bone.

Bring head back and away from hand (at a diagonal).

!

Hold each stretch for 20-30 seconds while taking deep breaths.

Make sure to repeat on the opposite side to ensure both sets of muscles are equally stretched.

upper trap stretch

The Upper Trapezius and Levator Scapula are essentially your "shrugging" muscles, or the "I slept funny" muscles. These muscles are tense more often than not. The following are targeted stretches that will help reduce tension in this area.

STEP 1

Bring right arm behind back.
Bring the opposite (left) ear to the (left) shoulder.

**Do not lift the shoulder to meet the ear.*

STEP 2

Turn face down to look at the ground.

**Do not lift the shoulder to meet the face*

Hold each stretch for 20-30 seconds while taking deep breaths.
Then switch sides.

This combo will effectively stretch both muscle groups - AND stealthily help you check if you applied deodorant that morning.
Now that's what I call a WIN-WIN!

arms & hands

You may not realise it, but you use your arms and hands a LOT.

If you work in an office, you probably do your fair share of typing and mouse clicking. Over time, you may experience tightness in the hands, arthritis in the joints and possibly carpal tunnel syndrome in the wrist.

What most people don't know is that their finger flexor and extensor muscles all attach at the elbow. So to effectively stretch the hands, you need to stretch the forearms.

Here's how you do it:

To stretch your flexor muscles, hold the arm out in front of you with your palm facing up, and using your other hand, pull the hand down.

To stretch your extensor muscles, hold the arm out in front of you, palm facing down. Using your other hand, pull the hand down.

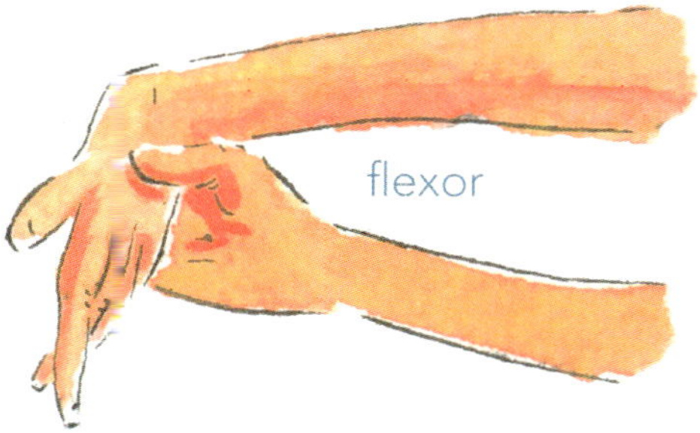

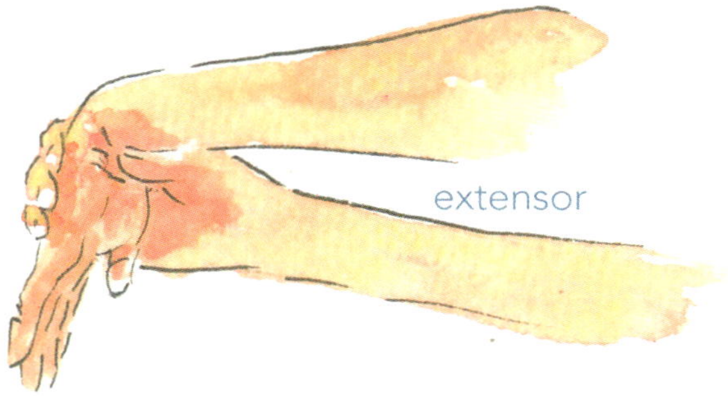

Hold each stretch for 20-30 seconds while taking deep breaths. Then switch sides.

carpal tunnel syndrome

Carpal Tunnel Syndrome is one of the biggest and most common pains associated with desk work.

It is a condition where the nerves that travel to the hands are pinched at the wrist. Over time, this pinching creates a chronic condition that causes increasing pain, burning or shocking sensations, and weakness and/or numbness felt in the hands.

If left unresolved, there is a risk of permanent nerve damage and a potential need for steroidal injections or even surgical intervention.

So to avoid Carpal Tunnel Syndrome, make your wrist health a priority.

Every day, practice these three things:

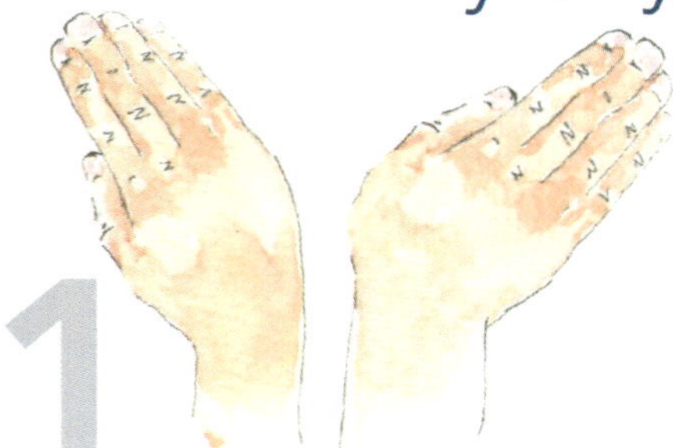

Wrist Mobility

Grip Strength

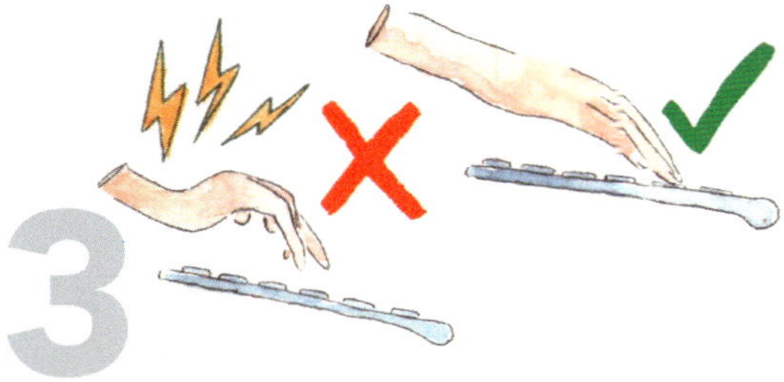

Proper Alignment

If these activities do not reduce carpal tunnel syndrome, consider getting a wrist brace, an ergonomic assessment and consulting a medical professional such as an acupuncturist or physiotherapist.

arthritis in the wrists & hands

Arthritis is a fancy word that describes inflammation and stiffness in the joints.

Most office workers and manual labourers will experience arthritis at some point in their lives. Over time, wear and tear and overuse of joints may cause arthritis. While there isn't currently a cure for arthritis, you can take steps to reduce the symptoms and prolong your joint health.

MY SOLUTION: A frozen water bottle.

Yep. Stick a water bottle in the freezer and TA-DA! You've got yourself a cold compress perfect for your arms and hands.

You see, cold helps to reduce inflammation, swelling and pain in the body.

By rolling your arms and hands with the hardened water bottle (ie. applying pressure onto the water bottle) you effectively stretch the muscles passively while the cold reduces pain, swelling and inflammation in the tendons and joints.

> **!** **Pro-tip:** Put a sock or two on your frozen water bottle to protect your skin from the ice.

When you've finished rolling out your arms and hands, stick the frozen water bottle back in the freezer for future use.

posture

Maintaining a healthy posture can be difficult, but it's worth striving for.

As mentioned in the Neck & Shoulders section of this book, if neglected over time, our posture worsens and can create one or both of these structural deformities:

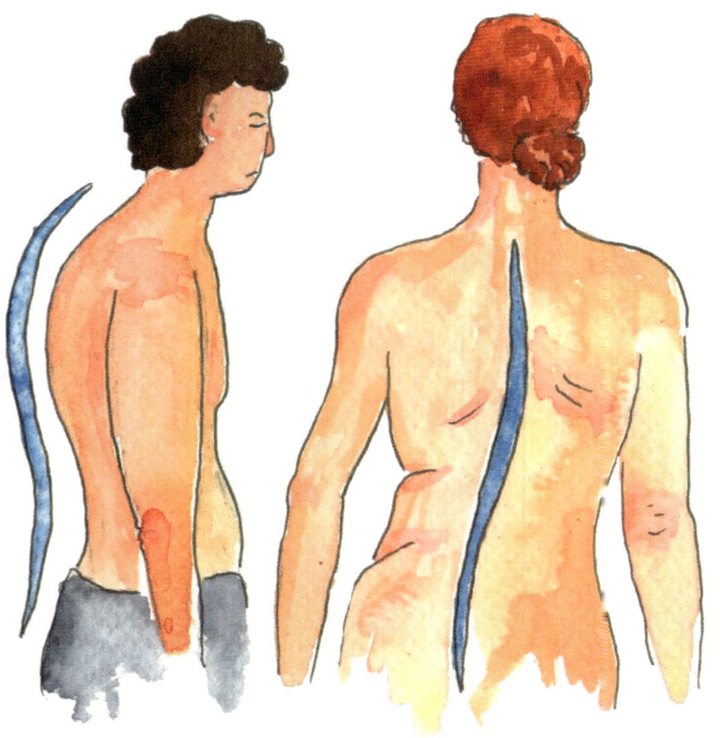

Disclaimer

To avoid these problems, you must first make a commitment to yourself. Posture is something that needs to be worked on regularly until it becomes a habit. Using memory triggers as reminders is probably the best method for making posture a priority.

postural habits

The following is a list of memory trigger opportunities to remind yourself to **sit up straight:**

- ✔ Red lights and stop signs
- ✔ When the phone rings
- ✔ Loading screens
- ✔ A knock at the door
- ✔ Waiting for the kettle
- ✔ Waiting in a queue
- ✔ Being in an elevator

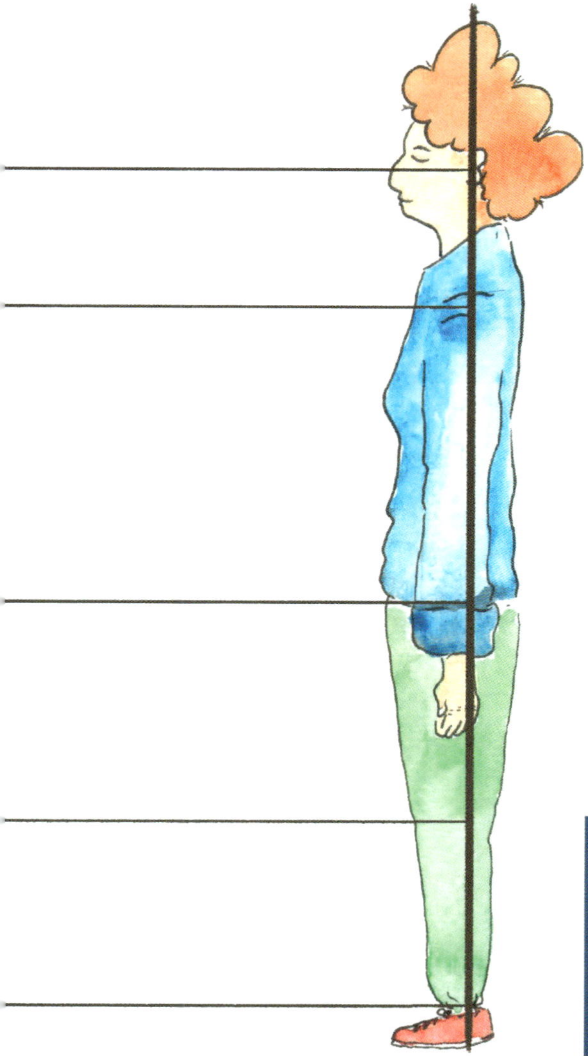

What's important is that your spine is straight.

This means aligning the ear with the shoulders and the hips.

I find it helpful to imagine a string coming from the ceiling, pulling at the top of my head.

Bring the shoulders back and down, keep the back straight and the head back.

Hold this posture consciously as long as you can.

This may be enough to help, but often poor posture is the result of muscular imbalance. This is where regular stretching and strengthening comes in.

Note: For professional help, seek out a credible ergonomics specialist, osteopath and/or chiropractor. They will help with proper alignment in ways you can't do on your own.

internally rotated shoulders the two-part solution

We do a LOT of things with our shoulders in an "internally rotated" position.

From typing to driving to crossing our arms and eating a sandwich... we pretty much live our lives in this position.

Over time, this position causes an imbalance in the upper body. This imbalance typically manifests as a tightness in the pectoral (or pec) muscles, resulting in weakened rhomboids, poor posture and back pain.

The solution?

Stretch your pecs and strengthen your rhomboids! Sounds complicated, but it's really not.

PART 1
pectotal stretching

STEP 1

Stand in a door frame.

Bring your arm up to meet the door frame.

STEP 2

Upper arm parallel to the ground.

Elbow bent 90°

Lean away.

Hold each stretch for 20-30 seconds while taking deep breaths. Then switch sides.

! It may be necessary to play with the angles of your arm to find the right stretch. You will know the stretch is done correctly if you feel a pull in the front of the shoulder and chest.

A similar stretch is done this way but with a straightened arm. This variation will stretch more bicep than pec. The bending of the arm will effectively cancel out the biceps and target pecs.

PART 2
rhomboid strengthening

Your rhomboids are the muscles between your shoulder blades.

When you squeeze the shoulder blades together, this strengthens the rhomboids. That's it. That's all you have to do - squeeze the shoulder blades together.

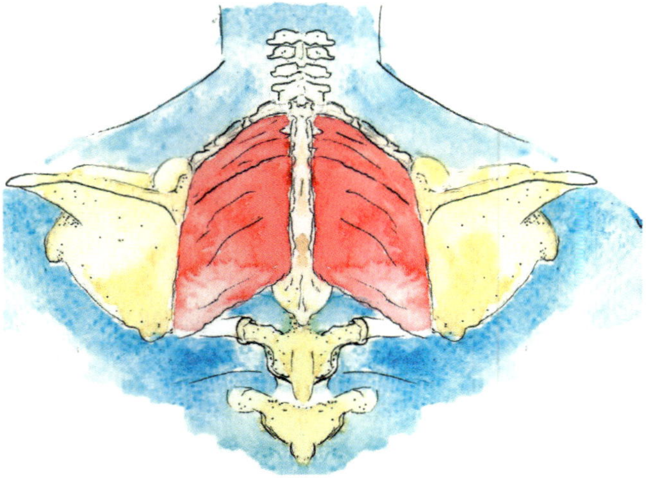

You can achieve this exercise by "cactusing" your arms like so.

Do this movement ten times, holding for a few seconds each time.

Attempt to bring the shoulder blades together.

Repeat three times each day.

core strength

Core Strength is everything. I exaggerate because it's nearly true.

Having a strong core can make such a significant impact on your life as a whole, that I consider it as important as staying hydrated and sleeping well.

Benefits of a strong core include:

- Less back pain
- Improved posture
- Better mobility and flexibility
- Stability and balance
- Lower chances of back injury
- Reduced chances of incontinence
- Better lifting abilities

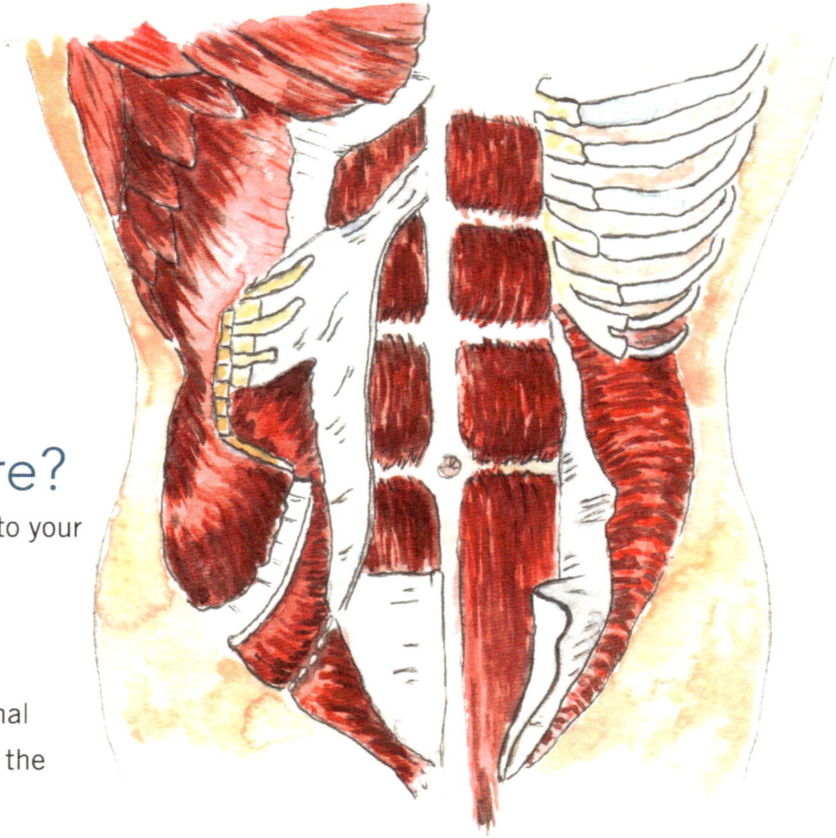

So... what **IS** your core?

Basically every muscle from your diaphragm to your pelvic floor. Your lats to your glutes and so much more.

This includes all your abdomen muscles, spinal muscles and all the muscles that encompass the pelvic girdle.

more than crunches

Crunches and abs do go hand in hand, but that's not the only path to a strong core.

Achieving core strength in the office could actually be pretty easy.

Solutions include:

> **NOTE:** If you aren't familiar with these exercises, maybe try a personal training session at your local gym.

back pain

Most people suffer with some form of back pain, usually in the upper or lower back. The following instructions mostly address lower back pain, as we have already covered upper back pain in the Neck & Shoulders section of this book.

Lower Back Pain can happen for any number of reasons, from poor sleeping posture, depression and menstrual cramps to muscle tightness in the quads or the back itself.

Most people carry tension in this area and it can be difficult to stretch. With that said, here's one stretch that's simple enough and can be done AT your desk.

lower back stretch

Follow these steps:

1. Sit in your chair facing forward, both feet firmly on the ground.

2. Cross your right leg over the left. (optional)

3. With a straight back, slowly turn your torso towards the right, attempting to look behind you.

Use the arm and back of your chair for leverage.

Hold each stretch for 20-30 seconds while taking deep breaths.

Then switch sides.

hip stretch

Your piriformis is an external rotator of the hip. This means it turns your leg outwards. When your piriformis is tight, it can lead to back pain, or worse, the dreaded sciatica.

This stretch requires a bit of flexibility and mobility in your clothing, but can be done almost anywhere.

Here's what you do:

1. Sit in your chair facing forward, both feet firmly on the ground.

2. Bend your knee, and bring that foot to the other knee.

3. Sit up straight.

4. Lean forward.

Hold your stretch for 20-30 seconds while taking deep breaths.
Then switch sides.

Note: A stretch should be felt in the buttocks and surrounding hip area. It is normal to also feel a pull in the back of the leg or hamstrings.

sciatica

Talk about a pain in the butt...

Of all the aches and pains, Sciatica has got to be one of the worst. Nerve pain in general is pretty agonising, but what's unique about the Sciatic is that it is THE largest nerve in the body, travelling out of the lower spine, into
the glute, down the leg and into the foot.

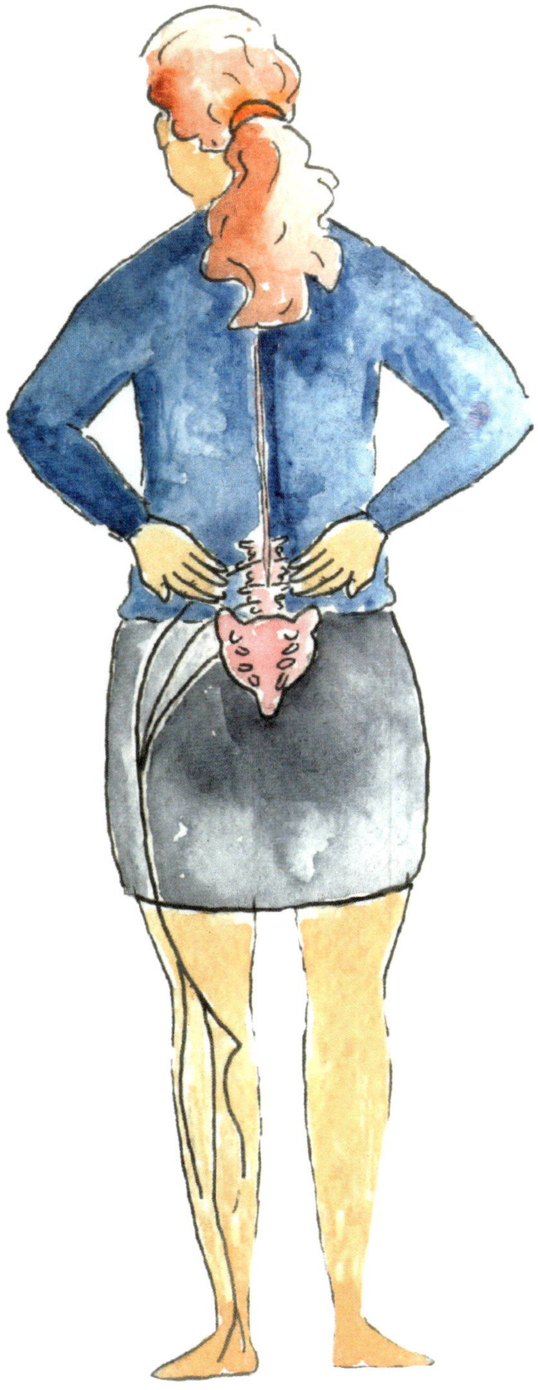

How it happens:

Between each of your spinal bones, or vertebra, there is a cushy disc whose role is shock absorption.

Sometimes, when lifting something heavy in an improper form, or in the case of traumatic sudden impact, the disc can be squished and become "prolapsed".

When this happens, the nerves become irritated and flare up in what is known as Sciatic pain or "Sciatica".

sciatica

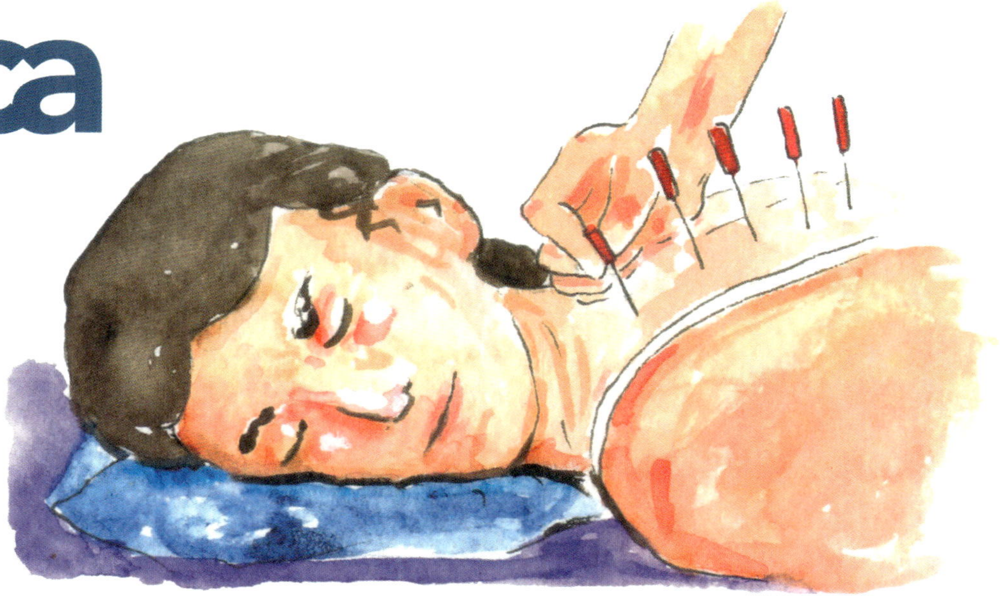

Sciatica is not a subtle pain. It is awful and unrelenting regardless of whether you sit, stand, lie down or hang upside down.

The pain is often felt as far down as the foot, and is accompanied by weakness, numbness and restlessness.

Unlike most pains that subside in a day or two, Sciatica if left unaddressed can last weeks if not months and is extremely difficult to resolve on your own.

So what do I suggest?

Get some professional help. My strategy includes a combination of acupuncture and kinesiology. For preventative measures: make sure you keep a strong core and have proper training in manual handling.

A WORD OF WARNING: Be careful with painkillers and anti-inflammatories. They may temporarily resolve the discomfort, but they may also lead to a false sense of security and further injury and aggravation. So take time off and get some help.

lower back pain

Life in the Fetal Position

A story about lower back pain

Your hip flexor muscles are some of the largest muscles in your body. Found on the front part of your upper leg, they are generally quite strong and can help or hinder you more than you know.

Having tight hip flexors is very common. It is especially prevalent in people who live life in the fetal position. What I mean by this is people who sleep on their side and have a sedentary lifestyle (sitting all day) between driving, work and home life (such as watching TV).

These people develop shortened hip flexors over time, because the muscles are constantly in a shortened position, a position of hip flexion.

As the hip flexors shorten over time, the pelvis is pulled out of optimal alignment, into what is known as

Lower Cross Syndrome.

lower cross syndrome

When the hip flexors become tight, they effectively pull on the front of the hips.

This is known as an 'Anterior Pelvic Tilt" and it results in what is known as 'Lower Cross Syndrome"

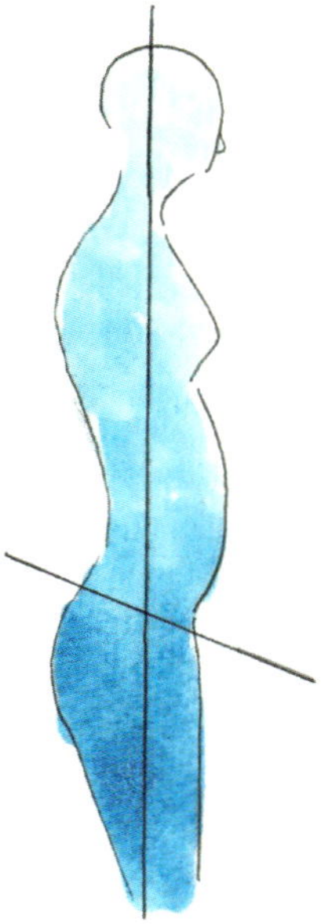

LCS is characterised by the following features:

- tight/shortened hip flexors
- weak glutes
- weak abdominal muscles
- tight/shortened low back muscles

Consequently this can lead to lower back pain and spasm.

So what can you do about it?

LCS solutions

The solutions are fairly simple in theory, but theory alone won't fix your lower back pain.

A standing desk is an ideal solution, as is stretching. Unfortunately, the following exercises are not so easily done at the office but they will help your lower back pain if done correctly.

stretch Hip Flexors

Treating them is easy.

1. Go down on one knee.
2. Keep a straight back.
3. Lean forward.

To increase the stretch, you can:

Grab the foot of the side being stretched.

OR you can lift the same side arm over head.

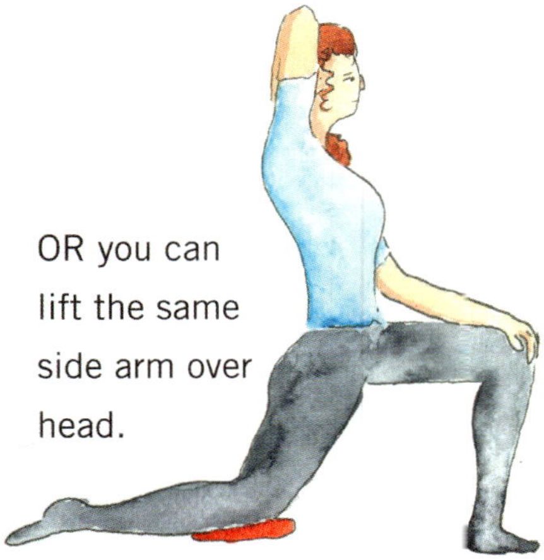

Hold your stretch for 20-30 seconds while taking deep breaths.

strengthen Abdomen & Glutes

Toning your abdomen and glutes is not just for superficial appeal, though seeing social media these days you'd probably think otherwise.

In reality, failing to tone your abdomen and glutes can be quite detrimental to your health and graceful aging. Core strength means stability, and stability means less likelihood of injury and chronic pain.

Here are some LCS resistant exercises to include in your exercise routine:

Squats

Planks

Bird Dogs

Bicycle Crunches

> **NOTE:** If you aren't familiar with these exercises, maybe try a personal training session at your local gym.

pillow talk

My last pro-tip for relieving lower back pain: a pillow.

Side Sleeper

If you're a side sleeper, keep a pillow between your knees while sleeping. This will balance the pelvic alignment and neutralise the spine.

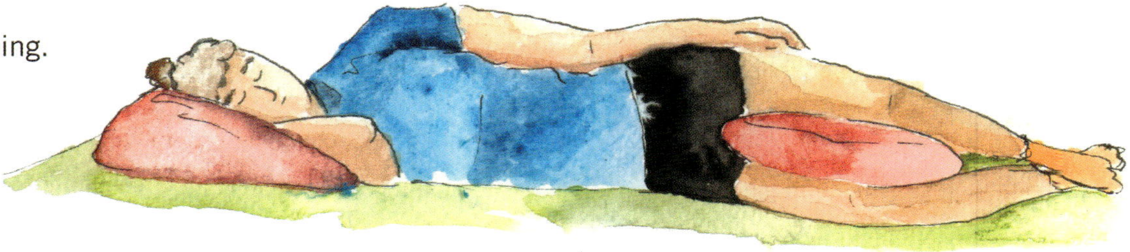

Back Sleeper

If you sleep on your back keep a pillow or two under the knees. This takes pressure off the lower back by neutralising the lumbar spine.

Front Sleeper

If you sleep on your stomach, STOP! Otherwise, sleep with a pillow under the abdomen and/ or lower legs. This also takes pressure off the lower back and neutralises the lumbar spine.

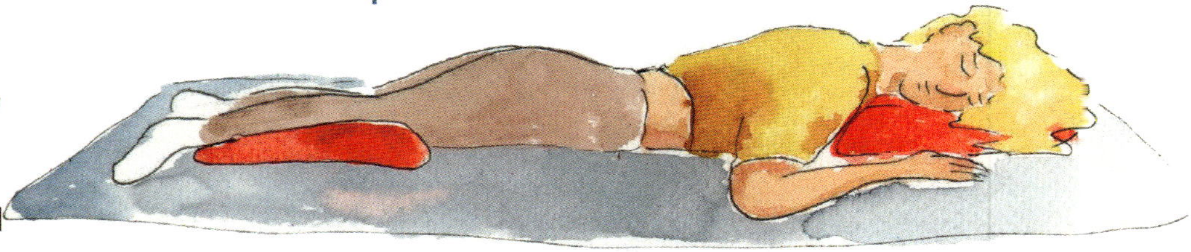

legs & feet

Having sore legs or feet is not ideal. Between weight bearing, walking and going up or down stairs, it's no wonder we get achy sometimes.

Stretching your legs regularly is highly recommended. Having flexibility is key to living a healthy and pain-free lifestyle and no one else is going to do it for you, so...

Start Stretching!!

REGULARLY

leg hands I mean FEET!

The feet are incredible structures, masterpieces of engineering, containing 26 bones and 33 joints each.

Taking care of your feet is one of the best things you can do for yourself.

Here are a few suggestions on HOW:

foot rollers

Remember that frozen water bottle we talked about in the arthritis page?

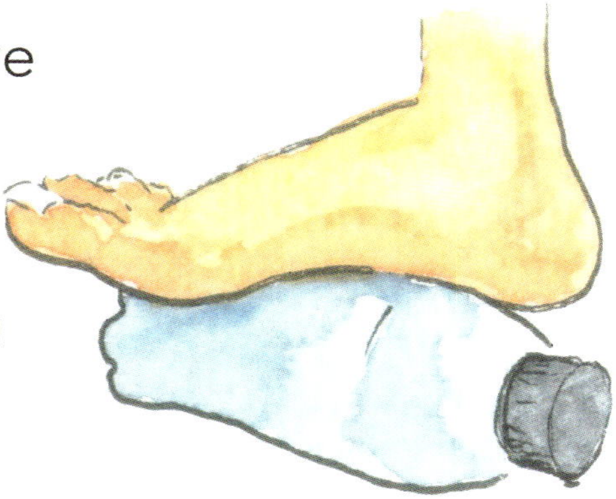

The one that may or may not already be in your freezer? Well, just as it helps your arms and hands, it will help your feet too!

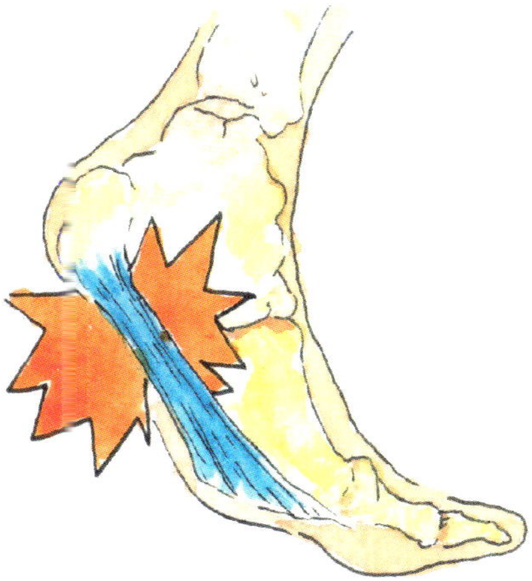

It will be especially helpful in the case of Plantar Fasciitis, which is defined as an inflammation of the tissue along the sole of the foot, connecting the heel to the toes.

It can be extremely unpleasant, characterised by heel pain and a burning sensation at the bottom of the foot.

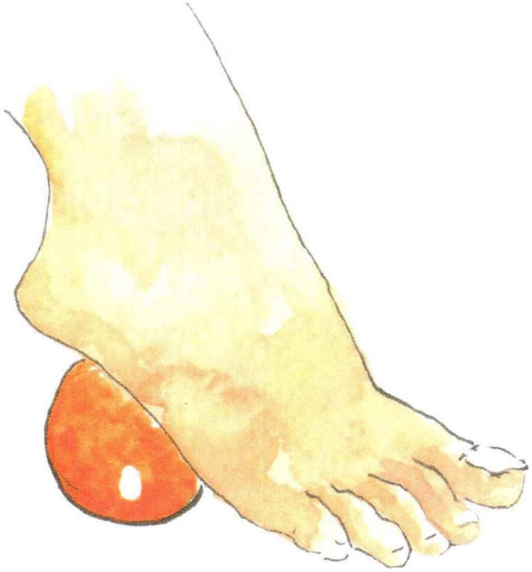

For more point specific self-care independent of freezers, try using a massage ball for the soles of the feet.

You can get them online, or even a simple tennis ball or a lacrosse ball will work.

I swear by this trick. It is magic.
And it can be done right at your desk!

self-care at home

Yes, this book is about self-care in the workplace, but I think it's my responsibility to tell you that you should also take this practice home too.

Self-care is ongoing and never ending. The less you resist it, and the more you infuse it into your life the better your overall quality of life will be.

If there was only one piece of home-based self-care advice I could give you, it would be this one:

contrast hydro

Contrast hydro at its core is alternating between hot and cold.

This is easy enough to do in the shower, especially if you're aiming for a full body effect. However, you can also localise it fairly easily. All you need is a hot water bottle or heat pad and a cold compress or even just a bag of frozen peas. Ice-water arm baths are a great solution too.

Why would I be suggesting this?

Well, there are many benefits to contrast hydro. From improving circulation and detoxifying the body, to strengthening your immune system, to easing depression and aiding in the cessation of smoking. You really can't go wrong.

The way you do it is simple. Apply heat for several minutes, then switch to cold for several seconds to a minute. The more you do it, the more you will enjoy the contrast, and the more your mind and body will benefit.

how much is too much

Addiction of any kind is not healthy, even when it comes to work.

Workaholism is a real problem and it's important to be honest with yourself and recognise if you are in fact addicted to work.

Everyone needs to make a living to keep a roof over their heads, but balance is key. A healthy work-life balance is achievable and it's best to take baby steps for permanent change.

Steps you can take toward a healthy work-life balance include:

Start & End Times

Morning Routine

Stretch Breaks

Social Outings

Finding a work-life balance is imperative to your mental health. With it you can avoid things like burn out, stress, insomnia and repetitive strain. Finding said balance leads to improved mental health and quality of life.

mental health

While I may have left this topic until last, it doesn't mean you should too.

It is just as important to maintain your mental health as it is your physical health.

The thing is,
people are slower to react to, or even acknowledge these conditions, because the "pains" associated with poor mental health aren't as outwardly obvious as physical pains can be.

anxiety & depression

Most people are familiar with these terms but they don't necessarily know how to recognise the symptoms and warning signs within themselves.

Pretty much everyone will experience anxiety or depression at some point in their life. Some are more prone to these conditions than others and there are many contributing factors.

Stress is most definitely one but so are life circumstances, hormone imbalances, poor diet and/or habits and a lack of exercise and self-care

Know the Signs

The following is a list of typical signs and symptoms of poor mental health.

anxiety

- Negative projections of the future
- Excessive worry
- Restlessness / irritability
- Being easily fatigued
- Increase / decrease in appetite
- Trouble concentrating
- Nightmares
- Sleep disturbance
- Muscle tension
- Nausea / stomach issues
- Feelings of fear
- Tightness in the throat or solar plexus
- Fast heart rate
- Inability to breathe / speak

depression

- Negative thoughts of the past
- Prolonged moodiness
- Feelings of emptiness or persistent sadness
- Lack of interest in enjoyable activities
- Increase / decrease in appetite
- Insomnia
- Oversleeping
- Lack of energy / feeling lethargic or apathetic
- Feelings of worthlessness
- Trouble concentrating
- Isolation / detachment
- Excessive weepiness
- Despair
- Suicidal thoughts

! **What to do about it?** Depending on the degree and severity of your symptoms, solutions range from a simple change in routine to medical intervention.

mental health solutions

There are many actions one can take to improve their mental health. Following are a few tried and true suggestions to infuse into your daily self-care routine:

More

- Water intake
- Deep breathing
- Meditation / Body scan
- Exercise
- Indoor plants
- Journaling
- Reading
- Goal Setting
- Tidiness of surroundings
- Artistic expression and music
- Healthy food
- Vitamins and minerals
- CBD oil
- Time spent in nature
- Quality time with loved ones
- Time spent with animals
- Dancing / Movement
- Counselling / Therapy
- Energy work and crystals
- Positive affirmations
- Aromatherapy
- Massage

Less

- Coffee
- Smoking
- Screen time
- Gossip
- Alcohol
- Recreational drugs
- Sugar
- Sitting
- Junk food
- Excuses
- Social media
- Television
- Hermiting / Hiding Away
- Procrastination
- Negative self talk
- Shoulda / Coulda / Woulda
- Feeling like the victim
- Time wasting
- Complaining / Blaming
- Comparing
- Clutter / Mess
- Expectations

The main driver of better self-care is a proactive and achievable self-care routine. If you can adopt an optimistic, glass half-full type attitude, your journey to mental healthiness will be much, much easier.

mental health exercises

A lot of mental health symptoms come from poor internal dialogue.

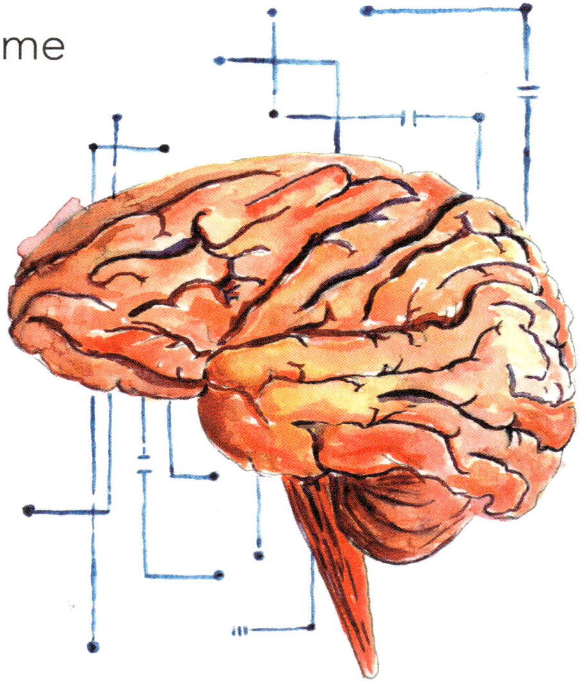

If your brain is a computer, your mind is the program, and mental health issues are like a virus or many viruses.

These viruses are the mental distortions and negative internal dialogue creating your reality.

Your consciousness is your malware. The more conscious, or present you are, the more you can pay attention to and filter what's being thought and said.

The following are examples of these negative thought patterns. Learn to recognise them, and you will be much healthier and happier.

thought patterns

1. **Black and white thinking:** This is the All or Nothing type mental process, one that is exclusive and resorts to extremes. Life is very much in the grayscale, and rarely an absolute.

2. **Taking things personally:** 99% of the time, people don't intend to hurt or alienate others with their words or actions, unless they are bullies. If you really feel targeted, seek to communicate and clear the air.

3. **Assumptions:** Jumping to conclusions rarely pays off. It is better to ask questions and search for answers, than to assume you know the truth.

4. **Expectations:** Similar to assumptions, but different. Expectation has an air of obligation, and often leads to disappointment. Instead, set intentions, but be open to the possibility that things may not always go as planned.

5. **Shoulda, Coulda, Woulda:** Try not to look back, after all, you're not going that way. Regret is heavy, and Shoulding all over yourself won't make the present any better. Forward action is the only way through.

6. **Mountains and Molehills:** Catastrophising an unfortunate event, or alternatively, minimising it, can really warp a sense of reality. Try getting outside perspectives and looking at things objectively.

7. **Self-Deprecation:** Negative self-talk, even if it's a joke, registers in the subconscious and takes a toll on your mental health. Be kind to yourself, and speak in affirmative language.

8. **Focusing on the negative:** Finding problems is easy. This life and this world have no shortage of things to complain about, but there is also an abundance of things to be positive about and be grateful for. Afterall, what's more pleasant? The silver lining or the gloomy cloud?

for some reason...

It is easier, and sometimes even more socially acceptable, to have destructive habits, like those in the "LESS" column, than to have constructive habits, like those in the "MORE" column.

It is said that your "vibe" attracts your "tribe" so be aware of the people you spend most of your time with, what it is they value and the habits they have.

Try to surround yourself with positive people who have common interests, healthy habits and long-term goals.

If you've done all this and still find yourself experiencing anxiety, depression or both, consult a therapist and then your doctor.

I am a passionate advocate for self-care and natural therapies first before pharmaceutical interventions, however in some cases medication may be necessary.

Should you choose to take medication for your mental health, please know there is nothing wrong with doing that. Just as people with poor eyesight may need glasses, so too might people with imbalanced hormones need help to rebalance them. Be patient, easy and loving towards yourself, because very often it is our own selves who can get in our way the most.

! These issues may not be resolved overnight but with prolonged and persistent effort, you CAN turn your mental health around and be healthy once more.

remember

Your mental health is important

Taking a **"mental health day"** is absolutely acceptable and even necessary.

No one expects you to be **100%** all the time and you shouldn't expect that of yourself either.

You are human, you have good days, you have bad days. This is inevitable and the sooner you learn to recognise the signs, the better you will be at treating the symptoms and resolving the issues.

There is nothing wrong with going to therapy, going to counselling, or needing medication. There is nothing wrong with admitting you aren't feeling your best or asking for help.

Be proactive, take care of yourself and rest before you're forced to. Self-care is a priority and a necessity, not a luxury. It's giving the world the best of you, not what's left of you.

outsourcing self care

Across the western world, employee wellness is being prioritised like never before. People are becoming comfortable with concepts like massage, guided meditation, acupuncture, counselling and yoga.

As the holistic realm gains traction and recognition, a supply of corporate wellness services are growing to meet demand. These on-site services come in the form of:

Chair Massage

Guided Meditation

Counselling & Coaching

Physical Exercise

OFFICE KNEADS

Office Kneads is a corporate wellness company founded by Giada Labrecque in Galway, Ireland that provides wellness services to corporates and organisations all over the country.

Our mission is to reduce stress, address aches and pains, and bring overall wellness into the workplace conveniently and effectively.

Our goal is to facilitate and provide corporate wellness services all over the western world.

Get in touch with Office Kneads at: www.officekneads.ie or e-mail: info@officekneads.ie

Michael Terence Publishing

First published in paperback by
Michael Terence Publishing in 2020

ISBN: 9781800940567

The information provided in this book is intended as a practical guide for self-care at work. It is not intended to diagnose, treat, cure, or prevent any condition or disease nor should it be used as a substitute for consultation with your doctor or licensed healthcare practitioner. The author is not responsible for any specific health needs that may require medical supervision and is not liable for any damages or negative consequences as a result of using the tips, tools and advice contained in this book.

Graphic Design: Design Associates
Illustration: Dmitri Nesterov

Printed in Great Britain
by Amazon

58261005R00030